KHAZAN SINGH V. UNION OF INDIA

VOLUME 2, ISSUE 2 OF BRILLOPEDIA

MRIDULA SHANKER

Contents

Preface

"Start writing, no matter what. The water does not flow until the faucet is turned on".

-Louis L'Amour

Hundreds of students and professors are contributing their work to Brain Booster Articles, we are here to provide ample information about Law and Contemporary issues. Our aim is to provide a platform for today's generation to express their views and ideas on law and contemporary law.

Author

CHAPTER ONE

Abstract

This paper examines the Khazan Singh v. Union of India case in great depth. In the present case, the petitioner filed a writ petition to challenge the validity of the court's decision to declare the petitioner's schedule caste certificate invalid because he was not born into the Julaha caste and was therefore ineligible to receive it. On the other side, petitioners asserted that because Kishan Lal did not have any children of his own, his biological parents gave him to Kishan Lal for adoption. He said that a deed of adoption and other traditional rites were performed on the day he was adopted, making him eligible to be considered as a member of the Julaha caste.

CHAPTER TWO

Facts

- Khazan Singh, the petitioner, is a former police sub inspector; he is a Jatt by caste as his father, a milk vendor, is from that caste.
- The petitioner alleges that he was adopted by Kishan Lal, a julaha by caste, because the petitioner's natural parents and adoptive parents agreed to give and take the petitioner in adoption into the family of Shri Kishan Lal because he had no offspring of his own.
- He further stated that on the day he was adopted, a deed of adoption was signed and certain customary rites were done; as a result, he is entitled to be treated as a member of the julaha caste, which is a scheduled caste under Article 341 of the constitution.
- The petitioners applied for a job as a sub inspector in the Delhi police service in 1971. He was asked to show his schedule caste certificate at the time of the interview. Following a thorough examination of the paper, the petitioner was appointed as a temporary sub inspector in the Delhi police service.
- However, on March 19, 1975, the assistant inspector general of police terminated his service, stating information that the petitioner was not born into the Julaha caste and hence was not eligible to receive the certificate mentioned above.
- On the 5th of April, 1976, an order was issued purporting to invalidate the certificate issued on December 26, 1970.
- So, the petitioner filed a writ petition challenging the order's validity dated April 5, 1976.

Issues

- Whether the adoption of the petitioner under Hindu Adoption and Maintenance Act, 1956 is valid or not?
- Whether the Schedule Caste certificate issued to the petitioner based on the adoption is valid or not?

Rules

- **<u>Section 12 of the Hindu Adoption and Maintenance Act</u>**

With effect from the day of the adoption, an adopted child is deemed to be the child of his or her adoptive father or mother for all purposes, and all links between the child and his or her birth family are deemed to be broken and replaced by those generated by the adoption in the adoptive family.

- **<u>Section 12(a) HAMA</u>**

A child cannot marry someone with whom he or she could not have married if he or she had remained in his or her biological family.

- **<u>Section 12(b) HAMA</u>**

Any property vested in the adopted child prior to the adoption shall continue to vest in such person, subject to any obligations arising from such ownership, including the need to maintain relatives in the family of his or her birth in the family.

- **<u>Article 341 of the constitution</u>**

This Article gives the President the authority to designate castes, races, or tribes as 'Scheduled Castes' under the Constitution. After consulting with the Governor of a State by public notification, the President is permitted to exercise this prerogative.

- **<u>Section 10 HAMA</u>**

Person who can be adopted— No person may be adopted unless the following conditions are met: i) he or she is a Hindu; (ii) he or she has not already been adopted; (iii) he or she has not been married, unless there is a custom or usage applicable to the parties that allows persons who are married to be adopted; and (iv) he or she has not reached the age of fifteen years, unless there is a custom or usage applicable to the parties that allows persons who are above fifteen to be adopted.

Analysis

- Respondent stated that because the petitioner was not born into a scheduled caste, he could not be treated as one, and that the certificate given previously was therefore erroneous and ought to be revoked. In Mrs. Urmila Ginda V. Union of India, learned counsel for the respondent relied strongly on the decision of Rangarajan J.In that case, the petitioner was a lady from a Punjab high caste family, married in 1969 a gentleman from the "adhann" community, who was a S. C., and the issue was whether she was eligible to be considered for a public office reserved for S. C., which she ran for in 1972. The learned judge pointed out that because the Hindu marriage Act removed all caste distinctions with regard to marriage, the petitioner became a sapinda of her husband who is a SC by virtue of their marriage, but gave answer in negative to the aforesaid question.

- In this instance, the court stated that the matter should be determined by considering not only the petitioner's impact on the adoption, but also the impact on future generations. The court went on to say that intermingling of castes and removing disparities between the forward and backward classes of society is a top priority in India today, and that in the long run, it may be found that the petitioner's main contention in this case is not really opposed to the constitution's object and scheme in regard to reservation for scheduled castes and tribes. On the other hand, if genuine adoptions in both directions become more common, the constitution's goal of social equality will be achieved. As a result, the court determined that the petitioner's certificate could not be revoked on the grounds that the petitioner's claim to be a scheduled caste by adoption was unfounded.

- The court stated that in the current situation, community consensus or acceptance is not required before a person can be admitted as a member of the cast. Because of his status as an adopted son, the adoptee becomes a member of the cast rather than an outsider seeking admission based on the good will and pleasure of the other members of the community. That rule only applies when admission is unavailable and must be given according to customary norms if the aspirant does not have a status sanction or birth right in his favour.
- Respondent cited section 10 of the Hindu Marriage Act, which states that a person who is to be adopted should not have reached the age of 15. This regulation can be relaxed if the parties have a tradition or usage that allows those who have reached the age of fifteen to be adopted. The court stated that it is not enough for the respondent to state that the petitioner was over the age of 21 when he was adopted; they must also state that this adoption was not permitted by customs, and that the petitioner should have been given an opportunity to prove that the adoption was valid before the certificate was cancelled.

CHAPTER SIX

Relevant Cases

- In the case of **Rangappa v. Chhannamma,**" the court held that after adoption, the child becomes a part of the adoptive family, and all links to his biological family are severed as of the day of adoption.
- The court decided in **Baban v. Parvati** that after adoption, the adopted father becomes the child's father and the adoptive mother becomes the child's mother. The adoptive son takes on the role of a natural-born child in the adoptive household after the adoption.
- In the case of **Basavarajappa v. Gurubasamma** it was said that "After adoption, the child is uprooted from his original family and transplanted into the adoptive family," His rights are equal to those of a natural child in every way. His natural family ties are severed, and he joins the adoptive family as a coparcener.

Conclusion

The court ruled that the adoptee should be treated as if he had been born into the adoptive family from the time of his adoption for all practical purposes. Except for the purpose stated in the section, he must forget that he is a member of another family from that day forward. As a result, his participation in that cast will be considered by birth.